▲ ART THERAPY COLORING

FLOWER
COLORING BOOK
FOR SENIORS VOL 2

Preview of Coloring Pages

www.arttherapycoloring.com

Did You Enjoy Our Coloring Book?

We Want To Hear About It!

Help spread the word about our adult coloring books! We give 10% of all proceeds from Art Therapy products to benefit pancreatic cancer patients and their families.

The best way to spread the word is through **Amazon reviews**. We know how busy you are, especially with all of that coloring, but we would appreciate it!

Visit our website at **www.arttherapycoloring.com**

with Love

Visit our website at www.arttherapycoloring.com

Get a Free Printable Coloring Ebook!

We've created an exclusive offer for our customers to receive a free Adult Coloring Ebook.

Visit **www.arttherapycoloring.com/freebie** to claim your free coloring book with over 30 new designs that you can instantly print and color!

Over 75 Anti-Stress Adult Coloring Books

See our collection of over 75 anti-stress coloring books for adults and teens on the following pages available at Amazon.com and other online retailers.

Art Therapy Adult Coloring Books

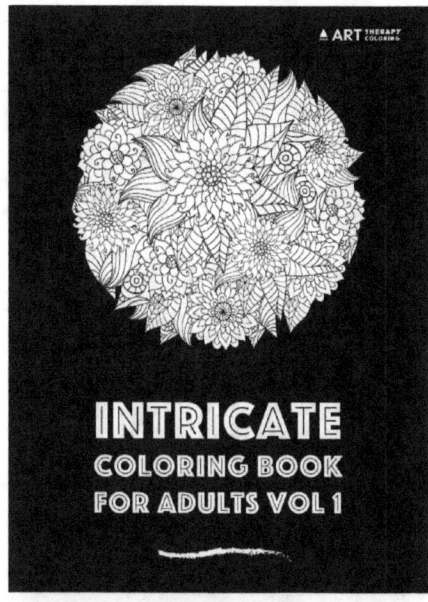

INTRICATE COLORING BOOK FOR ADULTS VOL 1

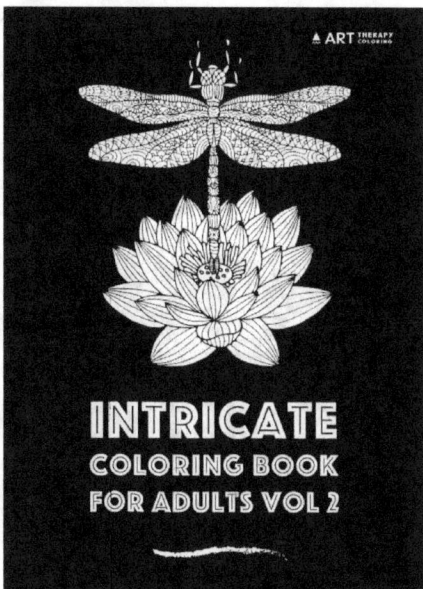

INTRICATE COLORING BOOK FOR ADULTS VOL 2

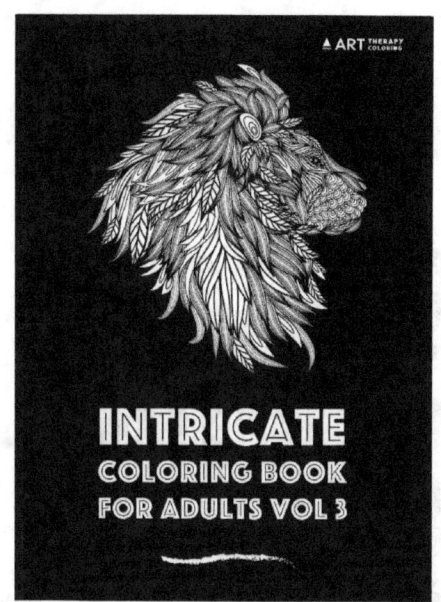

INTRICATE COLORING BOOK FOR ADULTS VOL 3

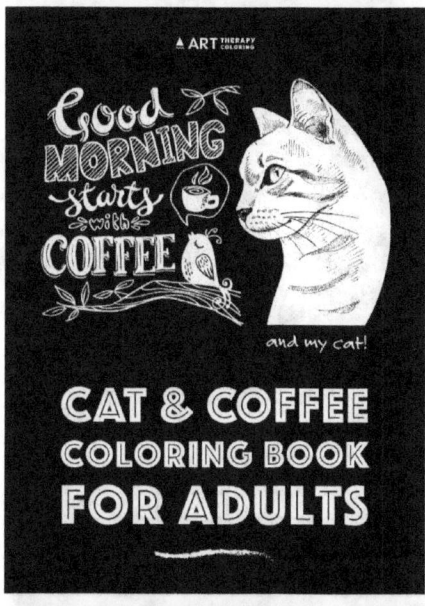

CAT & COFFEE COLORING BOOK FOR ADULTS

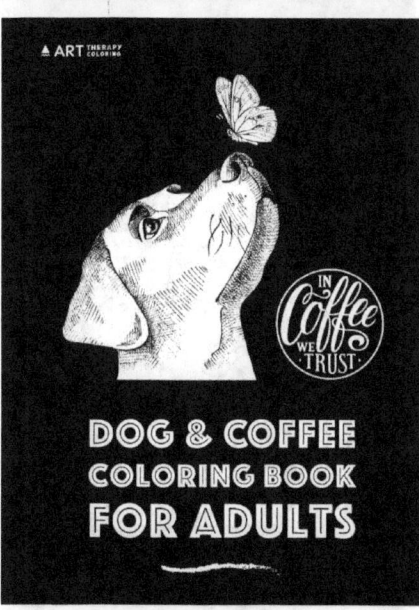

DOG & COFFEE COLORING BOOK FOR ADULTS

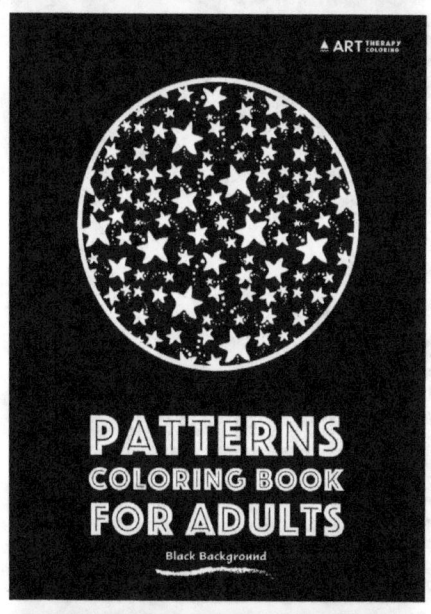

PATTERNS COLORING BOOK FOR ADULTS
Black Background

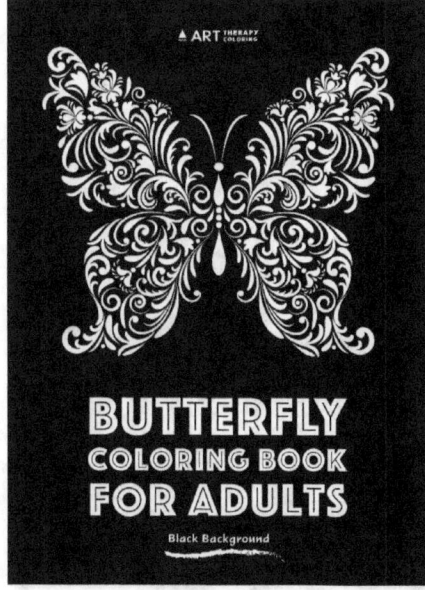

BUTTERFLY COLORING BOOK FOR ADULTS
Black Background

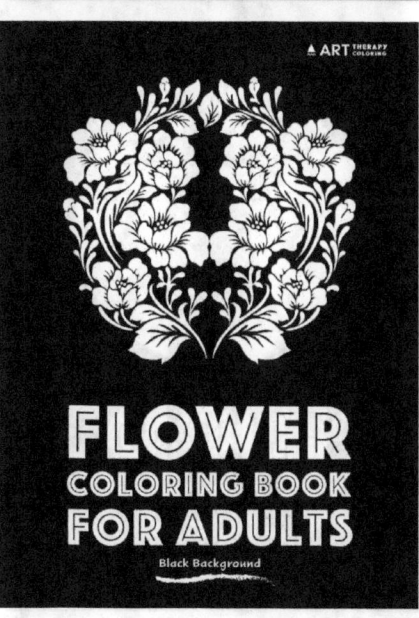

FLOWER COLORING BOOK FOR ADULTS
Black Background

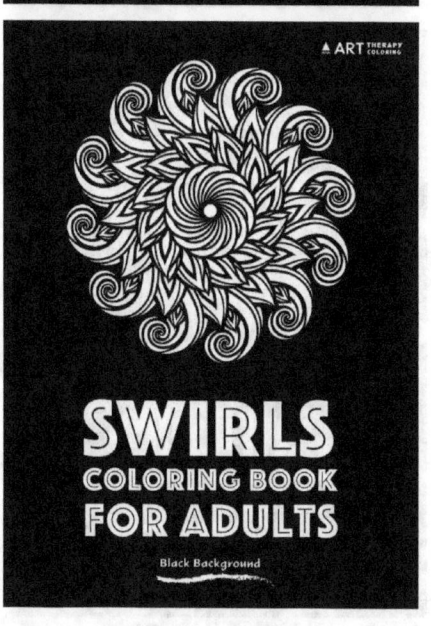

SWIRLS COLORING BOOK FOR ADULTS
Black Background

www.arttherapycoloring.com

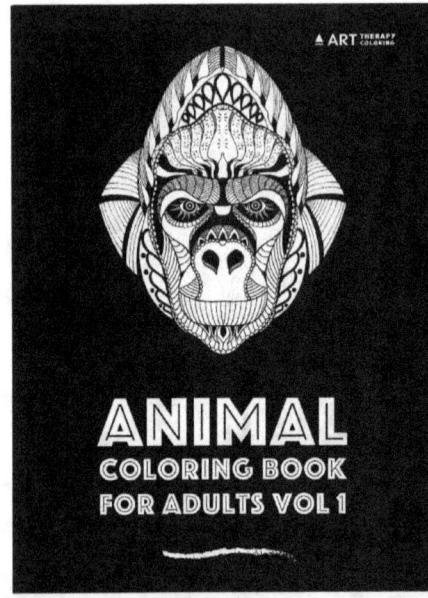

ANIMAL
COLORING BOOK
FOR ADULTS VOL 1

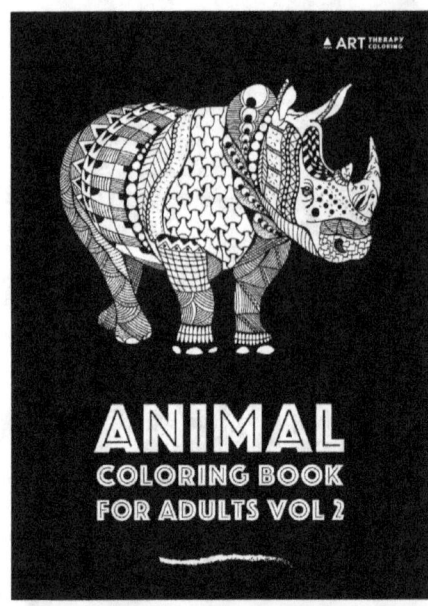

ANIMAL
COLORING BOOK
FOR ADULTS VOL 2

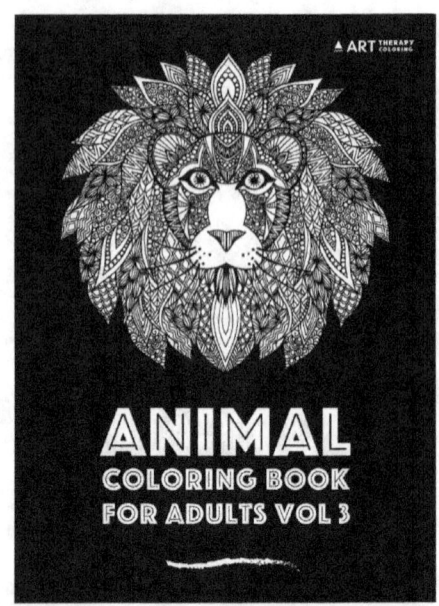

ANIMAL
COLORING BOOK
FOR ADULTS VOL 3

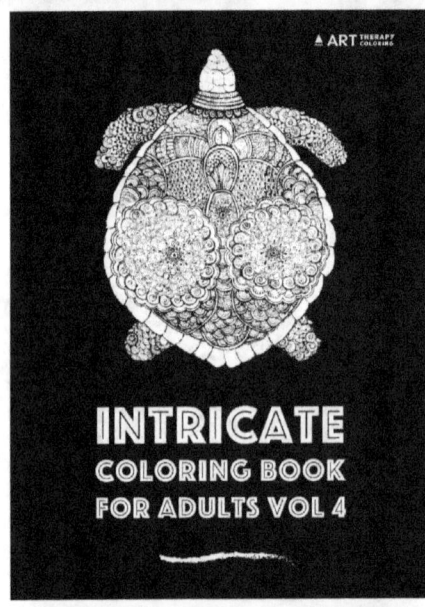

INTRICATE
COLORING BOOK
FOR ADULTS VOL 4

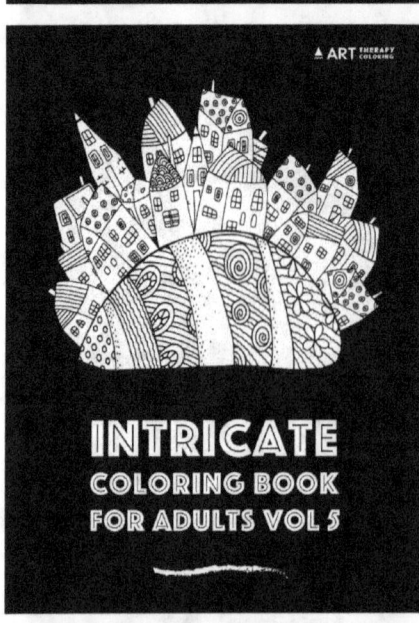

INTRICATE
COLORING BOOK
FOR ADULTS VOL 5

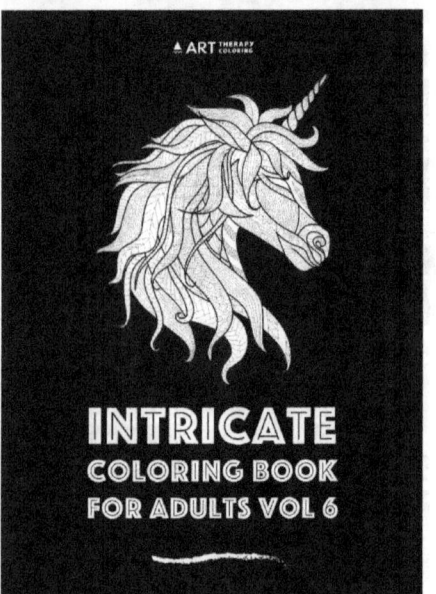

INTRICATE
COLORING BOOK
FOR ADULTS VOL 6

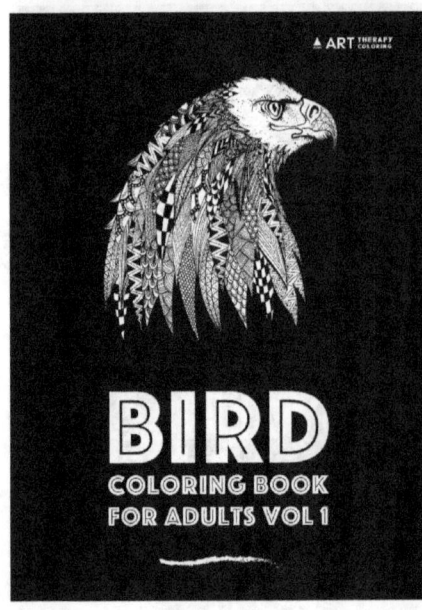

BIRD
COLORING BOOK
FOR ADULTS VOL 1

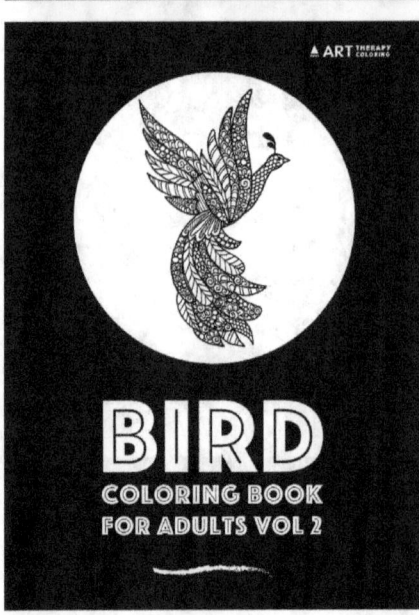

BIRD
COLORING BOOK
FOR ADULTS VOL 2

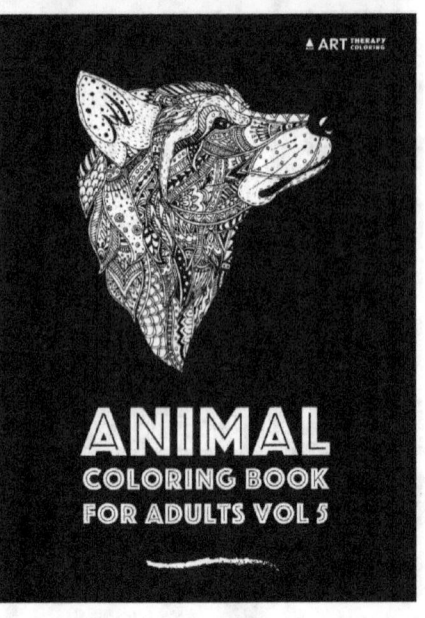

ANIMAL
COLORING BOOK
FOR ADULTS VOL 5

Art Therapy Adult Coloring Books

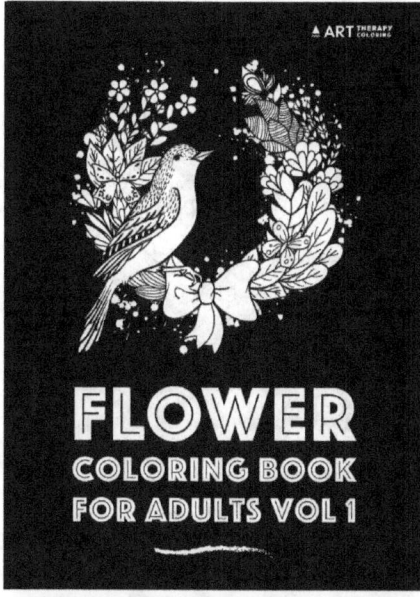

FLOWER
COLORING BOOK
FOR ADULTS VOL 1

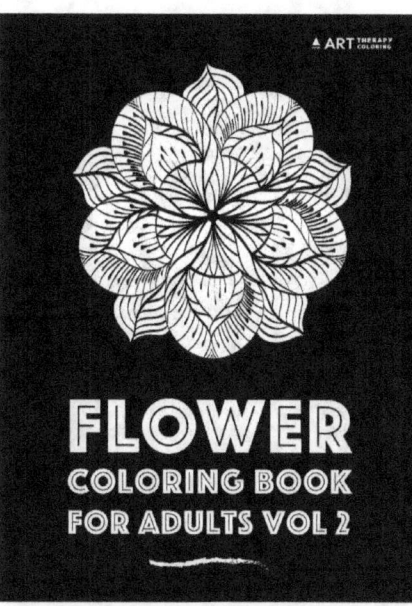

FLOWER
COLORING BOOK
FOR ADULTS VOL 2

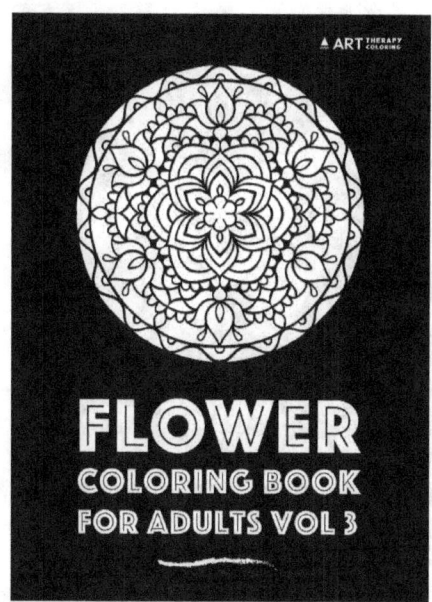

FLOWER
COLORING BOOK
FOR ADULTS VOL 3

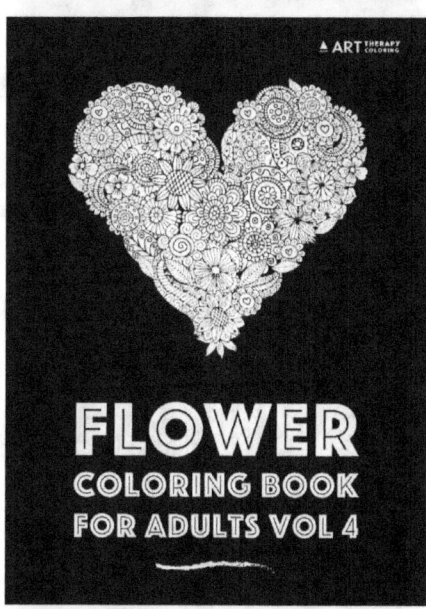

FLOWER
COLORING BOOK
FOR ADULTS VOL 4

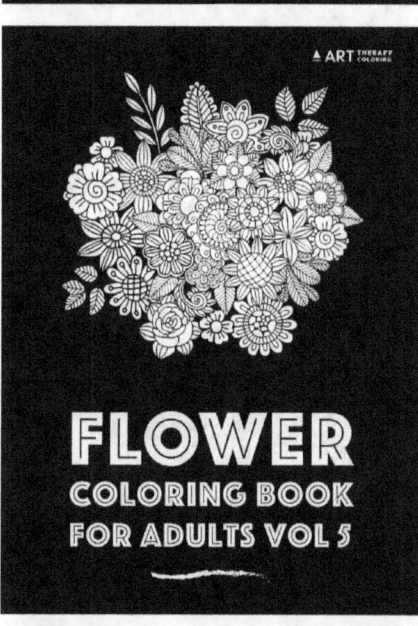

FLOWER
COLORING BOOK
FOR ADULTS VOL 5

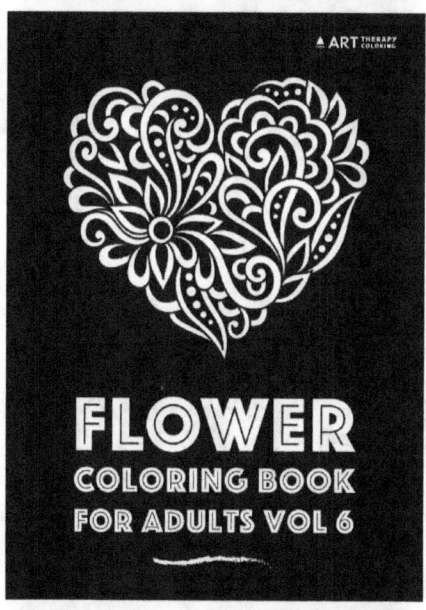

FLOWER
COLORING BOOK
FOR ADULTS VOL 6

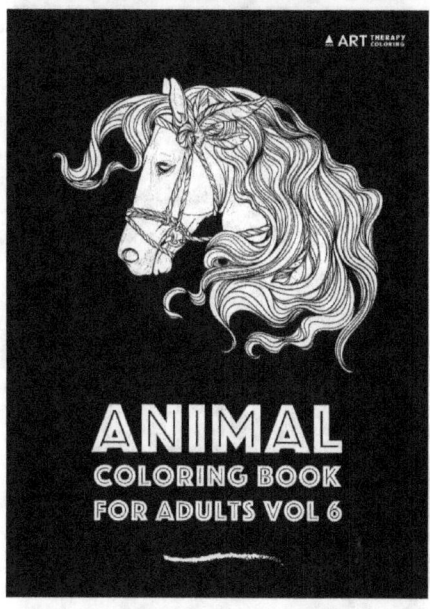

ANIMAL
COLORING BOOK
FOR ADULTS VOL 6

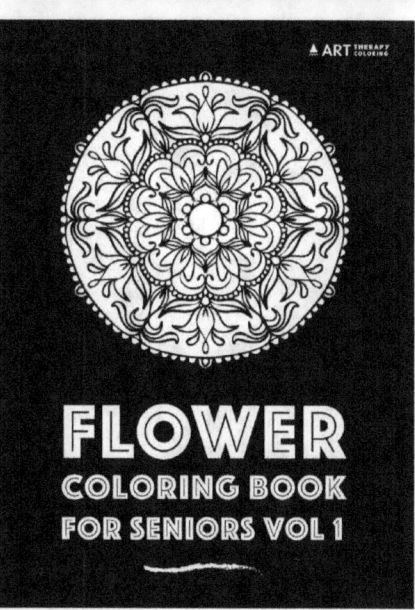

FLOWER
COLORING BOOK
FOR SENIORS VOL 1

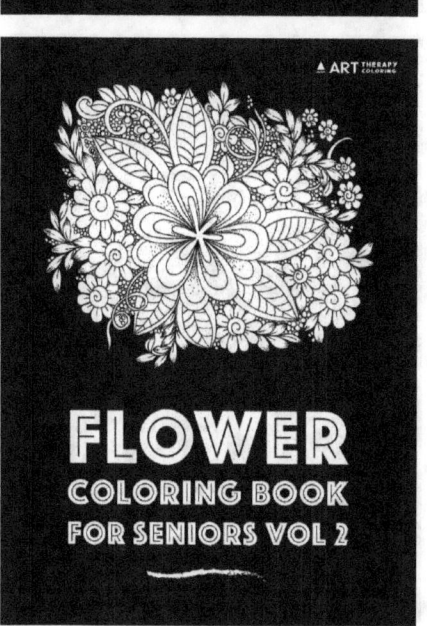

FLOWER
COLORING BOOK
FOR SENIORS VOL 2

www.arttherapycoloring.com

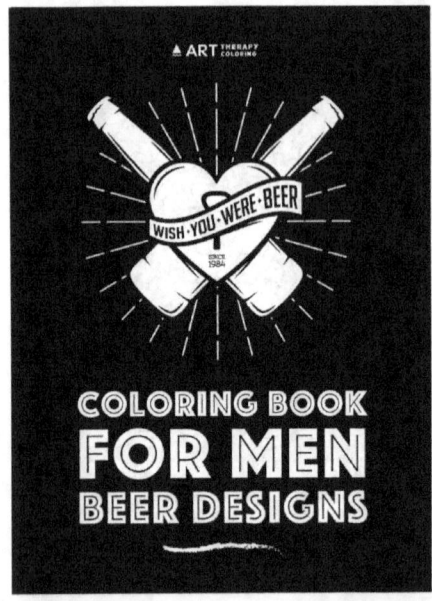

COLORING BOOK
FOR MEN
BEER DESIGNS

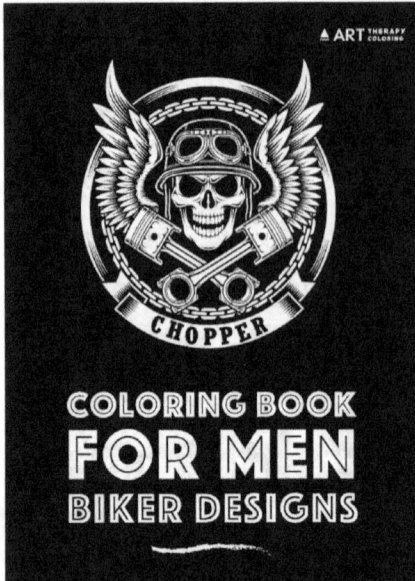

COLORING BOOK
FOR MEN
BIKER DESIGNS

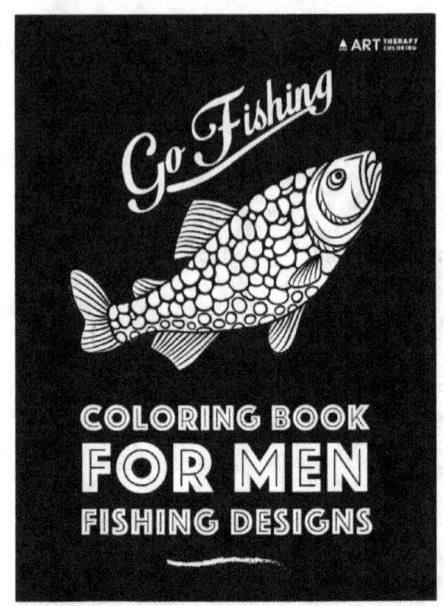

COLORING BOOK
FOR MEN
FISHING DESIGNS

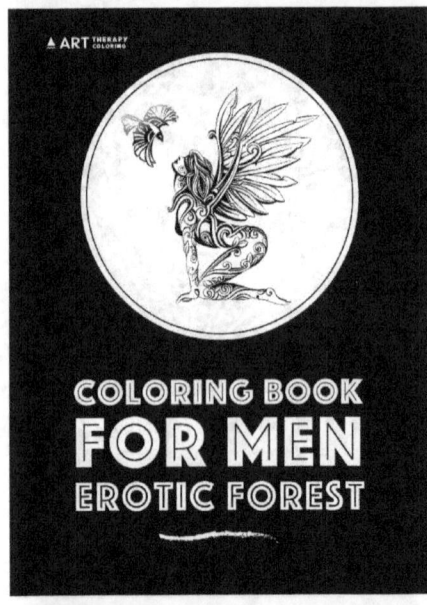

COLORING BOOK
FOR MEN
EROTIC FOREST

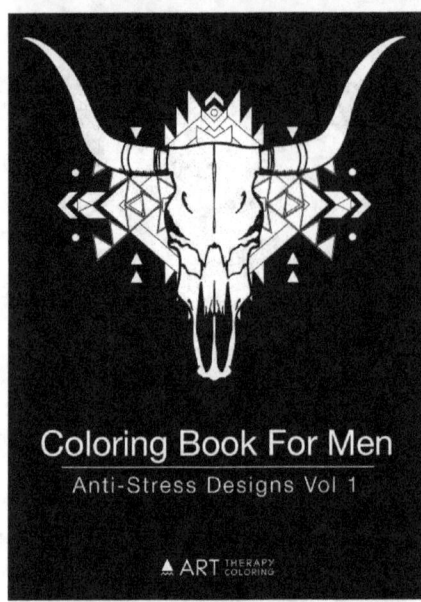

Coloring Book For Men
Anti-Stress Designs Vol 1

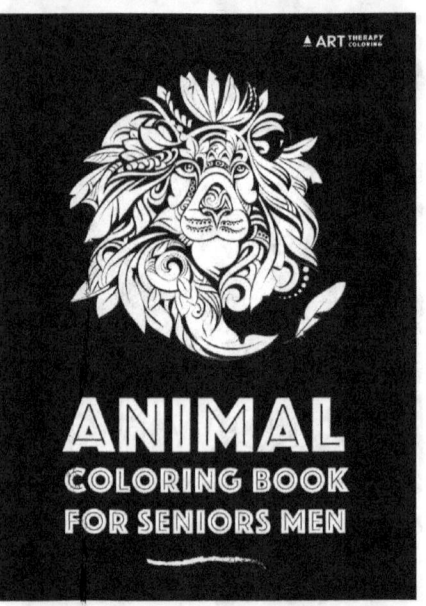

ANIMAL
COLORING BOOK
FOR SENIORS MEN

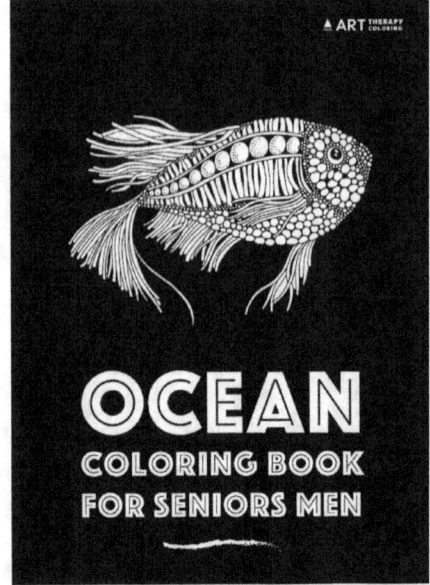

OCEAN
COLORING BOOK
FOR SENIORS MEN

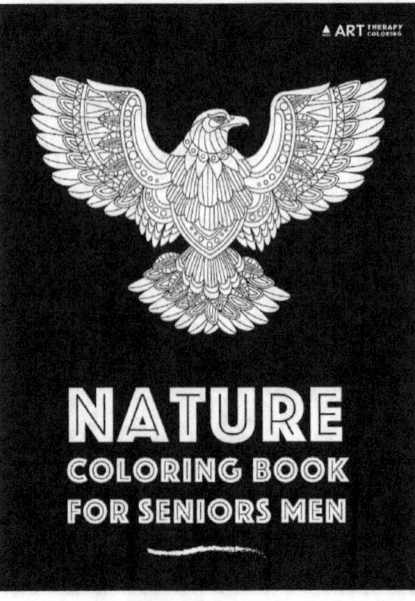

NATURE
COLORING BOOK
FOR SENIORS MEN

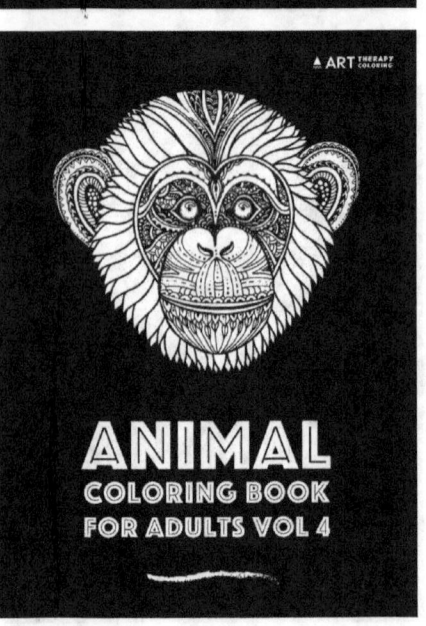

ANIMAL
COLORING BOOK
FOR ADULTS VOL 4

Art Therapy Coloring Books For Seniors

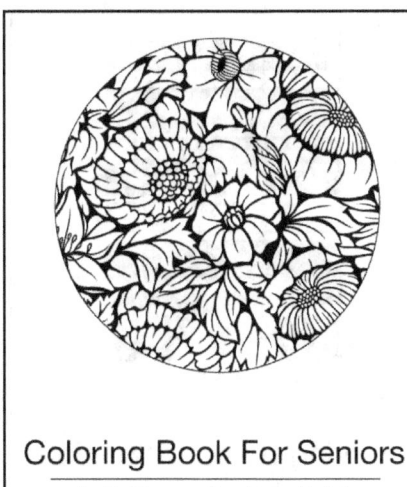

Coloring Book For Seniors
Anti-Stress Designs Vol 1

▲ ART THERAPY COLORING

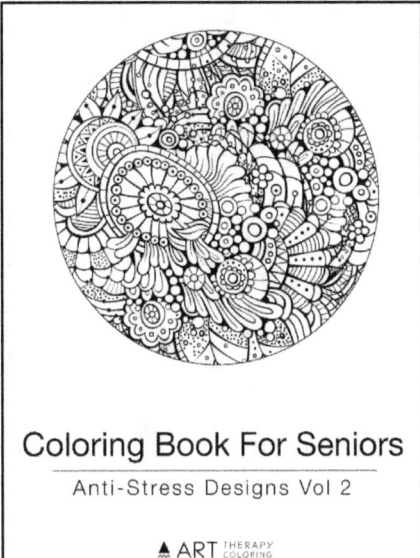

Coloring Book For Seniors
Anti-Stress Designs Vol 2

▲ ART THERAPY COLORING

Coloring Book For Seniors
Anti-Stress Designs Vol 3

▲ ART THERAPY COLORING

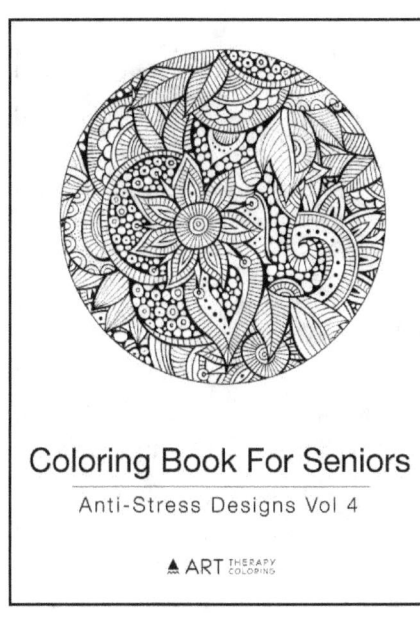

Coloring Book For Seniors
Anti-Stress Designs Vol 4

▲ ART THERAPY COLORING

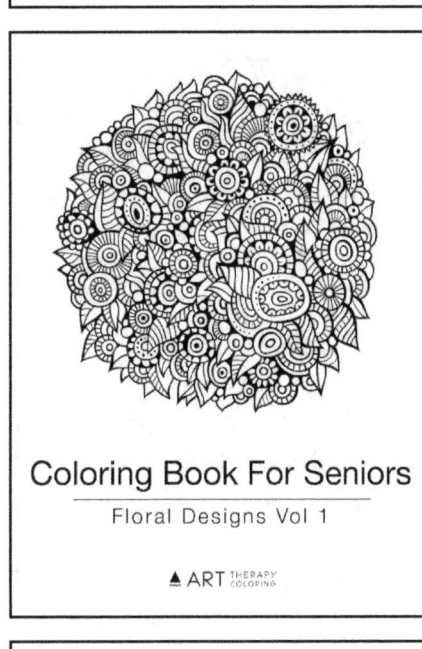

Coloring Book For Seniors
Floral Designs Vol 1

▲ ART THERAPY COLORING

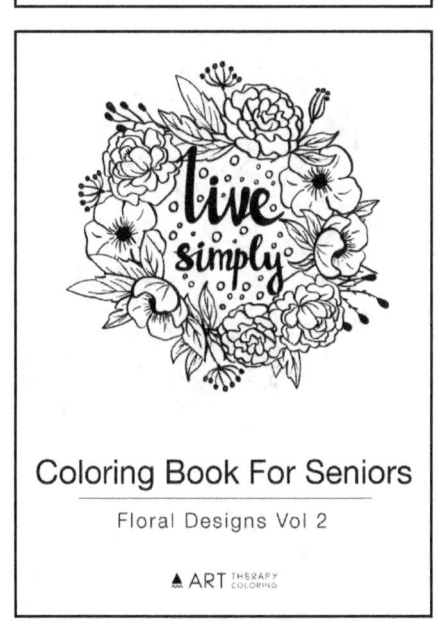

Coloring Book For Seniors
Floral Designs Vol 2

▲ ART THERAPY COLORING

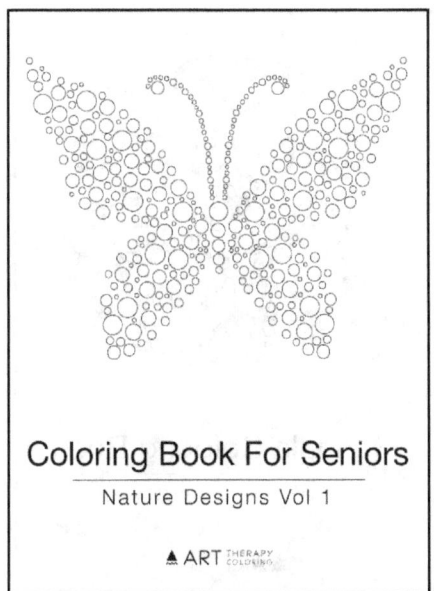

Coloring Book For Seniors
Nature Designs Vol 1

▲ ART THERAPY COLORING

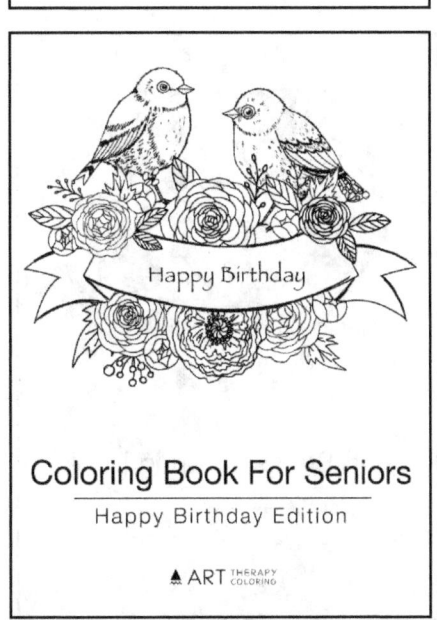

Coloring Book For Seniors
Happy Birthday Edition

▲ ART THERAPY COLORING

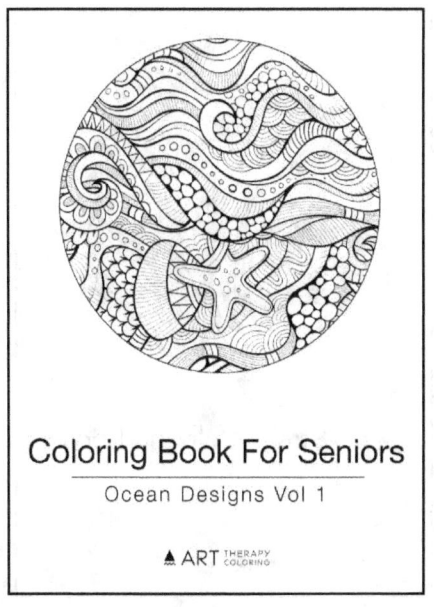

Coloring Book For Seniors
Ocean Designs Vol 1

▲ ART THERAPY COLORING

www.arttherapycoloring.com

Coloring Book For Seniors
Geometric Designs Vol 1

▲ ART THERAPY COLORING

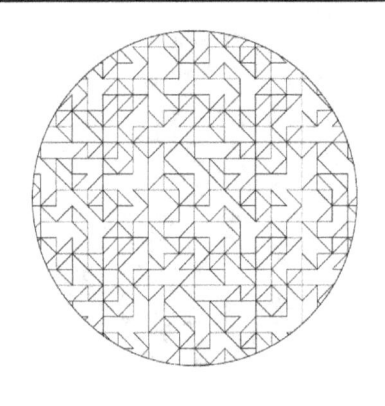

Coloring Book For Seniors
Geometric Designs Vol 2

▲ ART THERAPY COLORING

Coloring Book For Seniors
Geometric Designs Vol 3

▲ ART THERAPY COLORING

Coloring Book For Seniors
Nature Designs Vol 2

▲ ART THERAPY COLORING

Anti-Stress Coloring Book
Stress Relieving Designs Vol 1

▲ ART THERAPY COLORING

Anti-Stress Coloring Book
Stress Relieving Designs Vol 2

▲ ART THERAPY COLORING

Anti-Stress Coloring Book
Stress Relieving Designs Vol 3

▲ ART THERAPY COLORING

Anti-Stress Coloring Book
Stress Relieving Designs Vol 4

▲ ART THERAPY COLORING

Mandala Coloring Book
Stress Relieving Designs Vol 1

▲ ART THERAPY COLORING

Art Therapy Adult Coloring Books

Anti-Stress Coloring Book
Floral Designs Vol 1

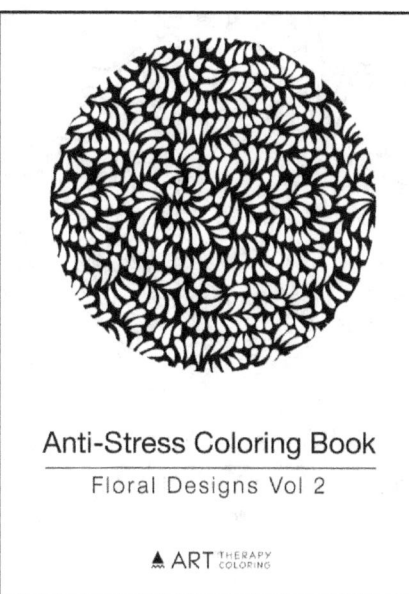

Anti-Stress Coloring Book
Floral Designs Vol 2

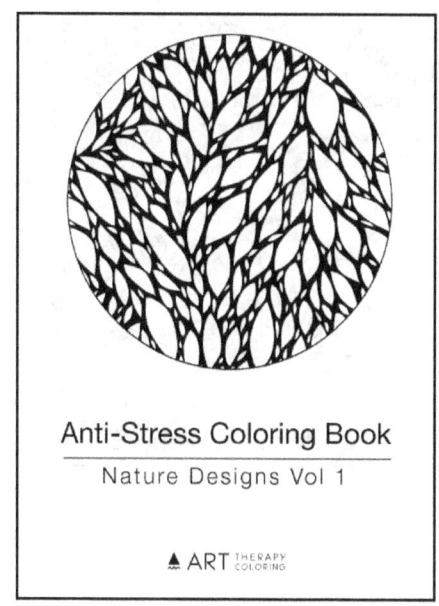

Anti-Stress Coloring Book
Nature Designs Vol 1

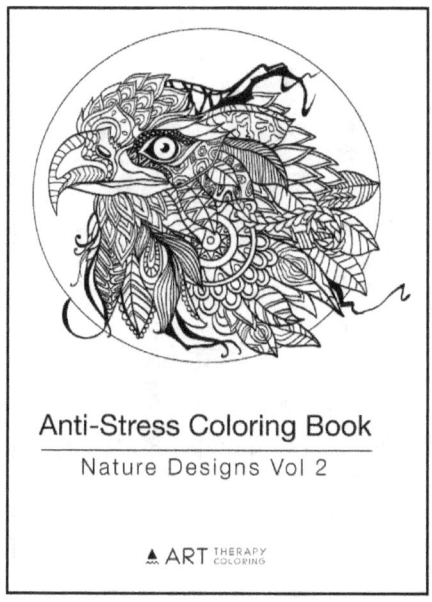

Anti-Stress Coloring Book
Nature Designs Vol 2

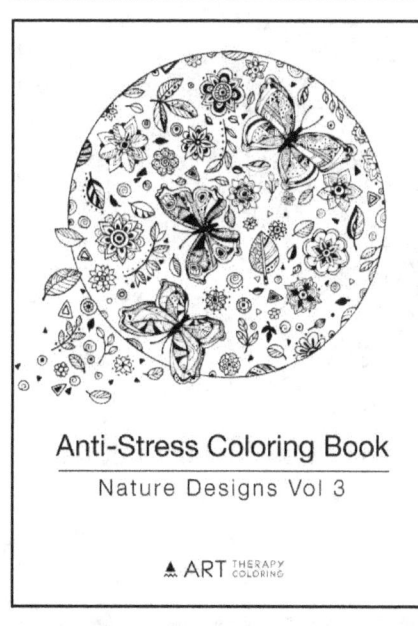

Anti-Stress Coloring Book
Nature Designs Vol 3

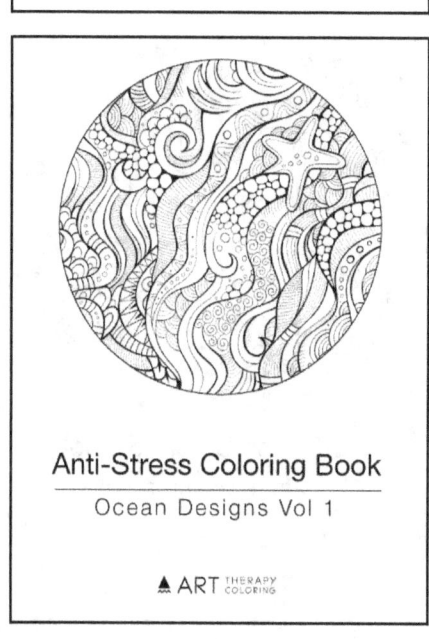

Anti-Stress Coloring Book
Ocean Designs Vol 1

Anti-Stress Coloring Book
Owl Designs Vol 1

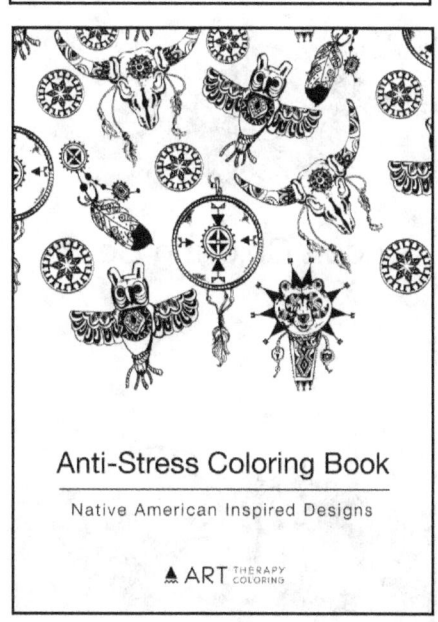

Anti-Stress Coloring Book
Native American Inspired Designs

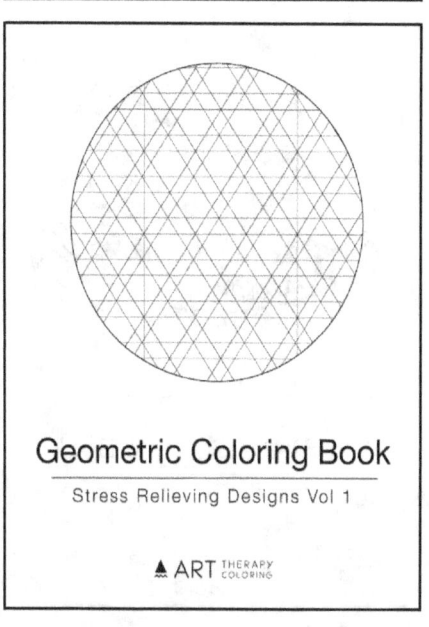

Geometric Coloring Book
Stress Relieving Designs Vol 1

www.arttherapycoloring.com

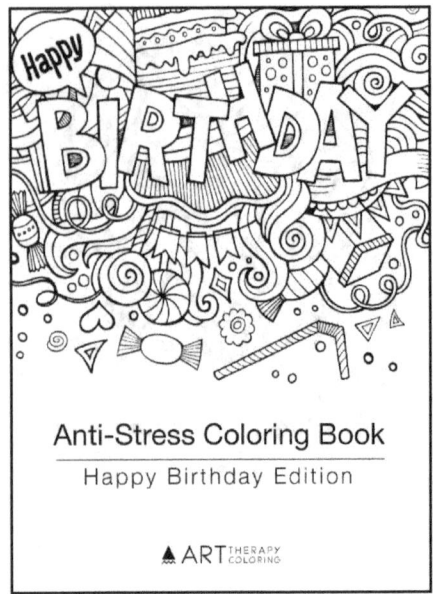

Anti-Stress Coloring Book
Happy Birthday Edition

▲ ART THERAPY COLORING

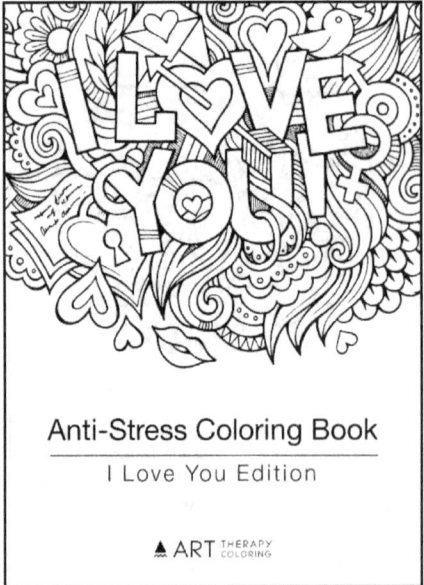

Anti-Stress Coloring Book
I Love You Edition

▲ ART THERAPY COLORING

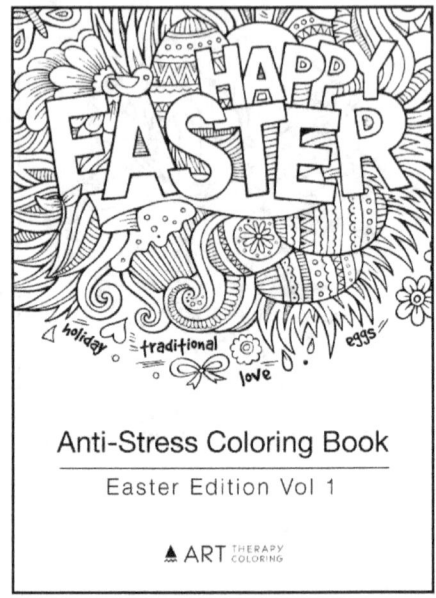

Anti-Stress Coloring Book
Easter Edition Vol 1

▲ ART THERAPY COLORING

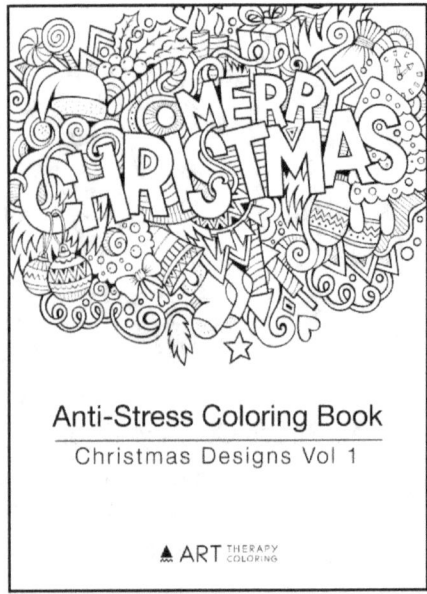

Anti-Stress Coloring Book
Christmas Designs Vol 1

▲ ART THERAPY COLORING

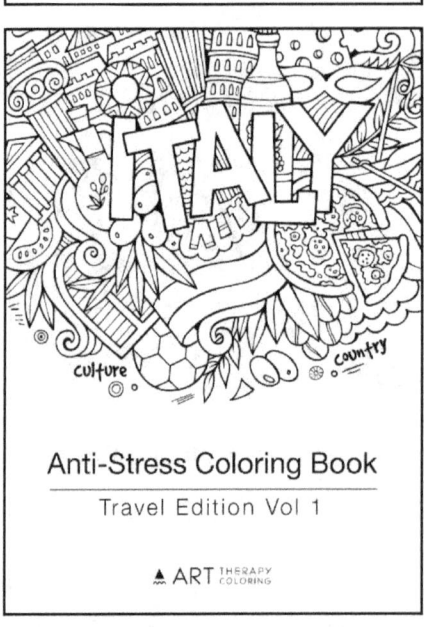

Anti-Stress Coloring Book
Travel Edition Vol 1

▲ ART THERAPY COLORING

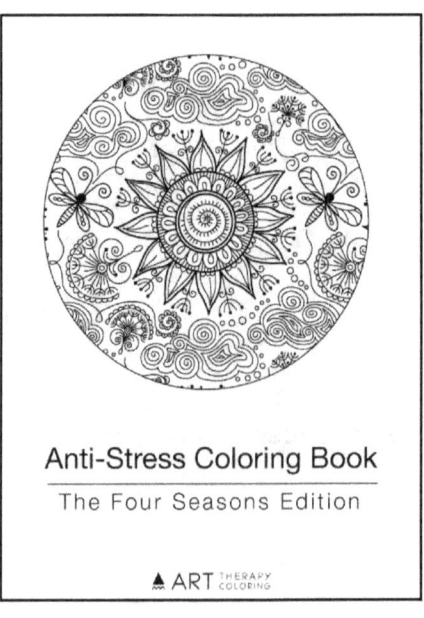

Anti-Stress Coloring Book
The Four Seasons Edition

▲ ART THERAPY COLORING

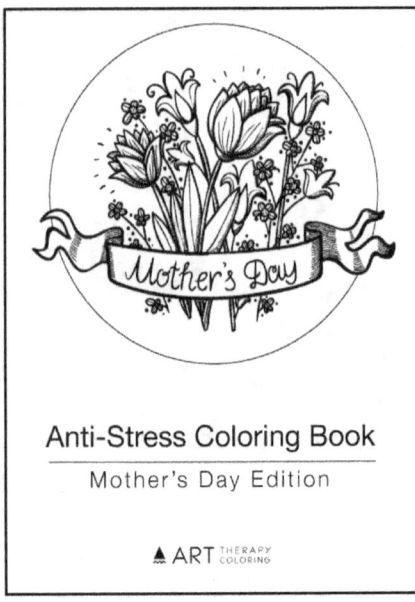

Anti-Stress Coloring Book
Mother's Day Edition

▲ ART THERAPY COLORING

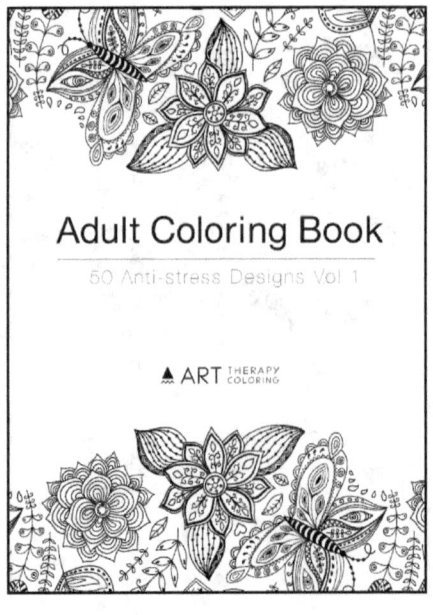

Adult Coloring Book
50 Anti-stress Designs Vol 1

▲ ART THERAPY COLORING

Art Therapy Coloring Books For Teens

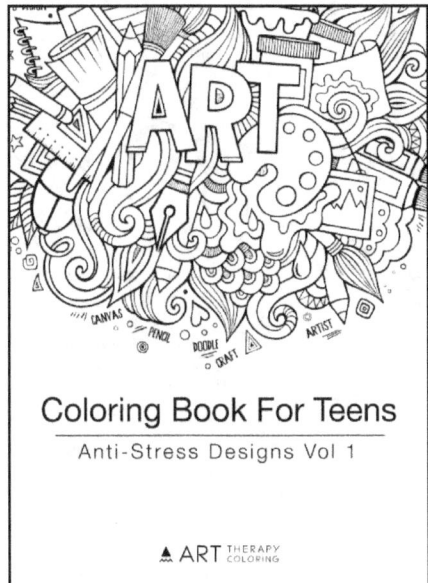

Coloring Book For Teens
Anti-Stress Designs Vol 1

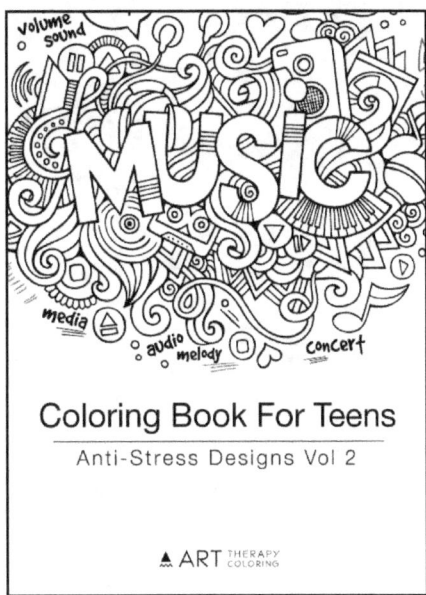

Coloring Book For Teens
Anti-Stress Designs Vol 2

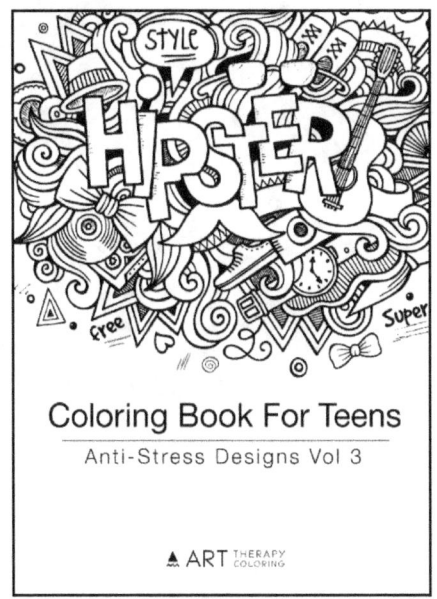

Coloring Book For Teens
Anti-Stress Designs Vol 3

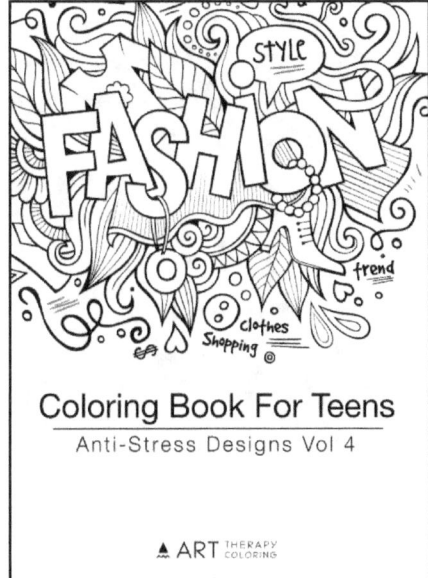

Coloring Book For Teens
Anti-Stress Designs Vol 4

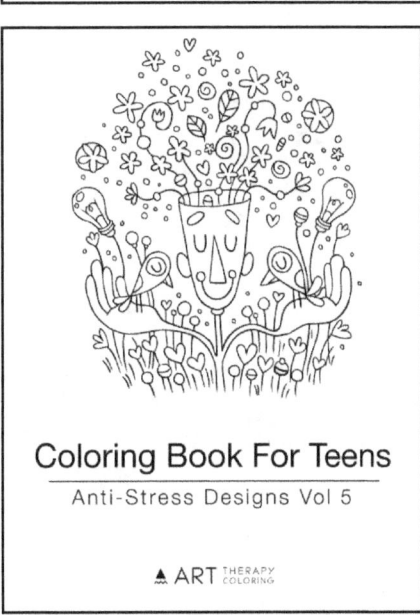

Coloring Book For Teens
Anti-Stress Designs Vol 5

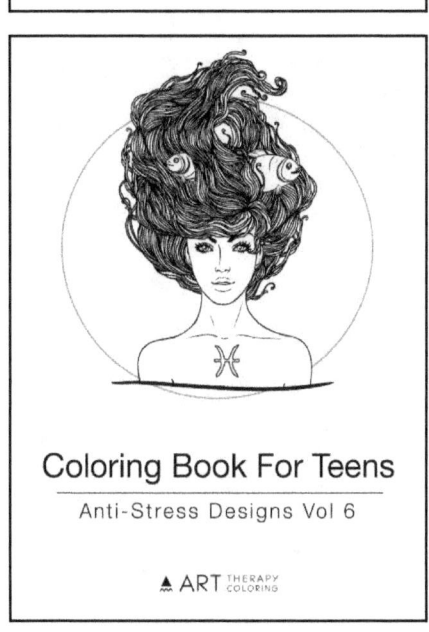

Coloring Book For Teens
Anti-Stress Designs Vol 6

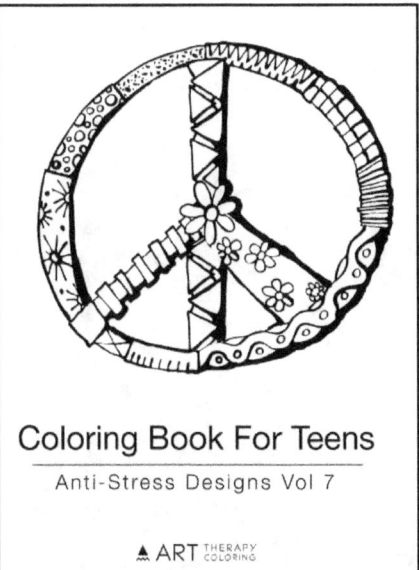

Coloring Book For Teens
Anti-Stress Designs Vol 7

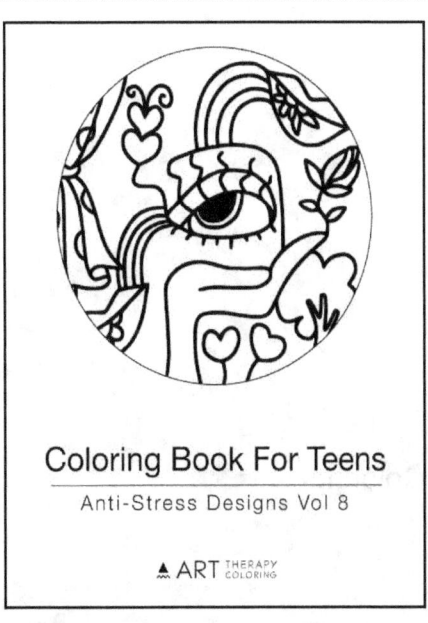

Coloring Book For Teens
Anti-Stress Designs Vol 8

Flower Coloring Book
For Seniors Vol 2

Published by:
Art Therapy Coloring
El Dorado Hills, California
www.arttherapycoloring.com

ISBN: 978-1-944427-76-4